TEAM SPIRIT ®
SMART BOOKS FOR YOUNG FANS

THE NEW YORK GIANTS

BY
MARK STEWART

New Hanover County Public Library
201 Chestnut Street
Wilmington, North Carolina 28401

NORWOOD HOUSE PRESS
CHICAGO, ILLINOIS

Norwood House Press
P.O. Box 316598
Chicago, Illinois 60631

For information regarding Norwood House Press, please visit our website at:
www.norwoodhousepress.com or call 866-565-2900.

All photos courtesy of Getty Images except the following:
SportsChrome (4, 12, 31, 32), Author's Collection (6, 20, 33, 37, 43 bottom),
Black Book Partners (8, 9, 10, 11, 14, 18, 19, 25, 35 top right and bottom, 39, 43 top, 45),
Bowman Gum Co. (15), Topps, Inc. (16, 21, 22, 26, 35 top left, 36, 40, 42 top),
Penguin Group USA (23), TCMA, Ltd. (34), National Chicle Co. (41),
Petersen Publishing Company (42 bottom), Matt Richman (48).
Cover Photo: AP Photo/Michael Perez

The memorabilia and artifacts pictured in this book are presented for educational and informational purposes,
and come from the collection of the author.

Editor: Mike Kennedy
Designer: Ron Jaffe
Project Management: Black Book Partners, LLC.
Special thanks to Topps, Inc.

Library of Congress Cataloging-in-Publication Data

Stewart, Mark, 1960-
   The New York Giants / by Mark Stewart.
      p. cm. -- (Team spirit)
   Includes bibliographical references and index.
   Summary: "Team Spirit Football edition featuring the New York Giants that
chronicles the history and accomplishments of the team. Includes access to
the Team Spirit website which provides additional information and
photos"--Provided by publisher.
   ISBN 978-1-59953-532-6 (library edition : alk. paper) -- ISBN
978-1-60357-474-7 (ebook)
   1. New York Giants (Football team)--History--Juvenile literature. I.
Title.
   GV956.N4S85 2012
   796.332'64097471--dc23
                                                    2012012314

Manufactured in the United States of America in North Mankato, Minnesota.
237R—082013

COVER PHOTO: David Bass and Bear Pascoe celebrate a touchdown
during a victory in 2012.

Table of Contents

ABOUT OUR GLOSSARY

In this book, there may be several words that you are reading for the first time. Some are sports words, some are new vocabulary words, and some are familiar words that are used in an unusual way. All of these words are defined on page 46. Throughout the book, sports words appear in **bold type**. Regular vocabulary words appear in ***bold italic type***.

Meet the Giants

At one time or another, every football team must live up to its name. For the New York Giants, that can be a tall order. It's one thing to be named after a bird or an animal. But there is a lot of pressure when you are supposed to tower over your opponents.

That is why the Giants are always looking for new ways to rise above the rest of the **National Football League (NFL)**. They do so with talent, hard work, and creativity. They take great pride in their past and in their future. The players love it when people call them "Big Blue."

This book tells the story of the Giants. Like all teams, they have had their ups and downs. New York has won glorious championships, and the team has lost games that its fans would rather forget. Yet through it all, the Giants always remember their goal—to stand head and shoulders above the competition.

Mathias Kiwanuka and Jason Pierre-Paul celebrate a good defensive play. They helped the team win a championship in 2012.

Glory Days

I n 1925, *professional* football was in grave danger. Millions of fans bought tickets each season to witness the daring feats of young college stars. However, sometimes only a few hundred people would show up for an NFL game. For Tim Mara, the owner of the New York Giants, this was a problem. His team played its first season in 1925, and empty seats were causing him to lose money.

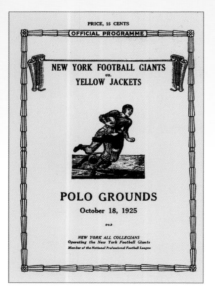

Mara believed that the NFL could—and would—do well in New York. That theory was put to the test in December of 1925 when the Giants hosted Red Grange and the Chicago Bears in New York City. Mara was thrilled when he walked onto the field and saw more than 70,000 fans in the stands. It was the turning point for the NFL and the Giants.

Beginning that *remarkable* day, the Mara family built one of the most successful teams in sports history. During the 1920s, the

Giants relied on a strong defense led by linemen Cal Hubbard, Al Nesser, and Steve Owen, who later became the team's coach. In 1927, New York

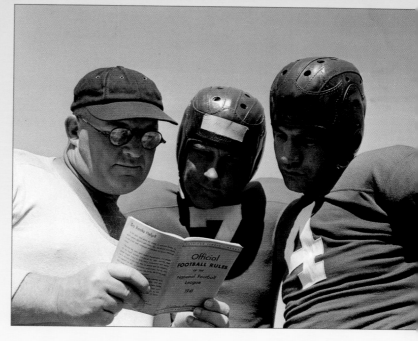

allowed only 20 points all season. With running back Jack McBride leading the offense, the Giants were crowned NFL champions.

In the 1930s, quarterbacks Benny Friedman and Harry Newman starred for New York. Their favorite targets included Ray Flaherty and Red Badgro. Ken Strong and Ward Cuff were among the best *all-around* players in the NFL. Another sensational Giant was Mel Hein. He was the only offensive lineman ever to be named the league's **Most Valuable Player (MVP)**. Hein was joined "in the trenches" by Frank Cope, Len Younce, and Al Blozis. The Giants won the NFL title in 1934 and 1938. They continued to field strong teams into the 1940s.

LEFT: This program is from the Giants' first season.   **ABOVE**: Coach Steve Owen checks out the NFL rule book with Mel Hein and Ken Strong.

7

During the 1950s and early 1960s, the Giants became the NFL's most glamorous team. They had many of the best-known stars in the game, including quarterbacks Charley Conerly and Y.A. Tittle, lineman Rosie Brown, running backs Frank Gifford and Alex Webster, and receivers Don Heinrich, Del Shofner, and Kyle Rote. The roster also included defensive stars Rosey Grier, Andy Robustelli, Sam Huff, Emlen Tunnell, and Jimmy Patton. The Giants won the NFL title in 1956 and played for the championship five times from 1958 to 1963.

After four **decades** of success, the Giants struggled to stay on top. From 1964 to 1983, they had just three winning seasons. During that time, the Giants moved from their longtime home in New York to the Meadowlands Sports Complex in New Jersey.

The Giants began to win again after the Maras turned to George Young to run the team's business affairs. Young made a great move when he hired Bill Parcells to coach the team. Parcells built a strong defense around linebackers Lawrence Taylor, Harry Carson, and Carl Banks. They held opponents in check, while quarterback Phil Simms put points on the board. He was surrounded by teammates

LEFT: Lawrence Taylor
ABOVE: Bill Parcells and quarterback Phil Simms talk over a play.

who played their best in big games, including running back Joe Morris and tight end Mark Bavaro. Under Parcells, the Giants won the **Super Bowl** twice, in 1987 and 1991.

The Giants continued to put top talent on the field in the years that followed. Receiver Amani Toomer, tight end Jeremy Shockey, and running backs Rodney Hampton and Tiki Barber were among the best in the NFL. The team's defense continued to shine thanks to Michael Brooks, Jesse Armstead, Keith Hamilton, and Michael Strahan. But without a great quarterback, the Giants fell short of another championship again and again.

In 2004, the Giants made a daring trade for Eli Manning. The Giants were convinced that he was the kind of leader who could get them back to the Super Bowl. Manning struggled at first, but as the years passed, Giants fans began to see that he was tough and talented. There was something special about him.

As Manning gained experience, the Giants refocused on their defense. It featured fierce tacklers and pass-rushers, including Osi Umenyiora, Justin Tuck, Antonio Pierce, Michael Boley, Corey Webster, Antrel Rolle, and Jason Pierre-Paul. In 2007 and again in 2011, the Giants made an exciting run through the **playoffs** and reached the Super Bowl.

Both times, the experts predicted that New York would lose. But Manning came through with amazing plays when all looked lost and led his team to thrilling victories. The Giants proved to a whole new *generation* of NFL fans that a team that plays together with intelligence and heart can accomplish anything if given the chance. It is a fact of football life that Giants fans have known since the 1920s.

LEFT: Eli Manning   **ABOVE**: Osi Umenyiora

Home Turf

For their first three decades, the Giants played at the Polo Grounds in New York City. In 1956, the team moved across the Harlem River to Yankee Stadium. The Giants stayed there until 1973. After two seasons at the Yale Bowl in Connecticut, the Giants played at Shea Stadium, the home of the New York Mets baseball team.

In 1976, the team moved into Giants Stadium, which was built in the New Jersey Meadowlands, a few miles from New York City. When that stadium got too old, it was knocked down, and the Giants opened a new home right next door. They share it with the New York Jets. When the Giants host a game, the stadium is decorated in their team colors.

BY THE NUMBERS

- The Giants' stadium has 82,566 seats.
- It cost $1.6 billion to build the stadium.
- The stadium is one of the most environmentally friendly in the NFL. It was made with more than 60,000 tons of recycled steel, and seats were made from recycled plastic.

Eli Manning takes the field at the team's stadium.

Dressed for Success

For most of their history, the Giants have worn uniforms with blue jerseys. That's how the team got its nickname, Big Blue. Red and gray have also been important team colors. During the 1950s, in fact, the team used red jerseys. In 2005, the Giants brought these uniforms back. Today, they like to wear their "throwback" uniforms on special occasions.

CHARLEY CONERLY

The Giants have featured blue helmets with a red stripe for much of their history. In 1961, they added a lowercase *ny* on the side. When the team moved to New Jersey, the old helmet **logo** was replaced by the word *GIANTS*. In 2000, the team switched back to its classic *ny* design. The Giants still use this helmet. Fans like it because it reminds them of the team's proud history.

LEFT: Corey Webster wears the Giants' home uniform.
RIGHT: Charley Conerly poses in the team's red jersey and helmet from the early 1950s.

We Won!

The Giants have won championships in seven different decades. Their first, in 1927, may have been their easiest. Back then, the team that finished with the best record was crowned the NFL champion. New York lost only one game that year and easily finished ahead of the Green Bay Packers and Chicago Bears.

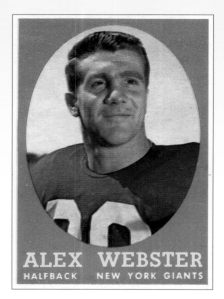

ALEX WEBSTER
HALFBACK   NEW YORK GIANTS

Starting in 1933, the top clubs from the east and west met in a title game to decide which team was the NFL's best. The Giants faced the Bears for the championship that season and again in 1934. They lost the first meeting but won the second. The 1934 game was played on an icy field in New York. The Giants trailed by 10 points in the fourth quarter, but Ken Strong and Ed Donowski led a comeback for a 30–13 victory. The Giants won it all again in 1938. They defeated the Packers thanks to two blocked punts and a leaping catch by Hank Soar for the winning touchdown.

New York fans had to wait until 1956 before they could celebrate their next championship. That season, New York beat the Bears 47–7 to win it all. Running backs Alex Webster and Mel Triplett trampled Chicago, while Charley Conerly connected with Frank Gifford on four passes for 131 yards.

New York's next championship came 30 years later. That season, Phil Simms and Lawrence Taylor helped the Giants set a club record with 14 victories during the regular season. They whipped the Washington Redskins and San Francisco 49ers in the playoffs, and then beat the Denver Broncos 39–20 in Super Bowl XXI. Carl Banks led New York's hard-hitting defense with 10 tackles.

The team's next trip to the Super Bowl was not as easy. The Giants started the 1990 season on a roll, but then Simms was injured. He was replaced by Jeff Hostetler, who had started only a few games in his career. New York advanced to the playoffs and faced the San Francisco 49ers for a chance to go to the Super Bowl. The Giants won 15–13 on a last-second **field goal**.

In Super Bowl XXV, they met the high-scoring Buffalo Bills. The Giants held a slim 20–19 lead in the final minutes. Buffalo moved the ball into New York territory with time running out, but the game-winning field goal sailed wide right. The Giants had their second Super Bowl championship.

New York returned to the Super Bowl in 2008. Brandon Jacobs and Ahmad Bradshaw led a punishing running attack that got even better in the **postseason**. The Giants won three playoff games on the road to advance to Super Bowl XLII. There they faced the undefeated New England Patriots. New York did not score a touchdown in the first three quarters, but the defense slowed down the Patriots. With New

York trailing 14–10 in the fourth quarter, Eli Manning completed a desperate pass to David Tyree in New England territory. Moments later, he tossed the winning score to Plaxico Burress for a 17–14 victory.

In 2011, the Giants were at it again. Their run to the championship was almost identical to the one they made four years earlier. New York got hot at the end of the regular season and rolled into the playoffs. The Giants advanced to Super Bowl XLVI for a rematch with the Patriots.

Once again, New York trailed late in the fourth quarter. Manning led the team on an 88-yard touchdown drive that featured an incredible pass to Mario Manningham. Bradshaw scored the winning touchdown to give the Giants a 21–17 victory and their eighth NFL championship.

LEFT: Brandon Jacobs powers through a hole against the Tampa Bay Buccaneers.
ABOVE: Mario Manningham waits for an Eli Manning pass.

Go-To Guys

To be a true star in the NFL, you need more than fast feet and a big body. You have to be a "go-to guy"—someone the coach wants on the field at the end of a big game. Giants fans have had a lot to cheer about over the years, including these great stars ...

THE PIONEERS

CAPTAIN

MEL HEIN

MEL HEIN   Offensive Lineman/Linebacker

- BORN: 8/22/1909   • DIED: 1/31/1992
- PLAYED FOR TEAM: 1931 TO 1945

Mel Hein was a great blocker and tackler and one of football's most athletic players. He was named the NFL's best center from 1933 to 1940 and was league MVP in 1938.

CHARLEY CONERLY   Quarterback

- BORN: 9/19/1921   • DIED: 2/13/1996   • PLAYED FOR TEAM: 1948 TO 1961

Charley Conerly was booed so often by the New York fans in the early 1950s that he almost retired. Coach Jim Lee Howell talked him into coming back, and Conerly led the Giants to the NFL championship. In 1959, Conerly was the league's top-rated passer and was named MVP.

FRANK GIFFORD — Running Back/Receiver

- BORN: 8/16/1930   • PLAYED FOR TEAM: 1952 TO 1960 & 1962 TO 1964

Frank Gifford was one of the most *versatile* players in team history. He was a good runner and receiver, an accurate passer, and an excellent pass defender. Gifford was so talented that he could even kick field goals.

SAM HUFF — Linebacker

- BORN: 10/4/1934   • PLAYED FOR TEAM: 1956 TO 1963

Sam Huff was a great leader and fierce middle linebacker. No matter where the ball was, he always seemed to be around it. The Giants played for the NFL title six times during his eight years in New York.

Y.A. TITTLE — Quarterback

- BORN: 10/24/1926   • PLAYED FOR TEAM: 1961 TO 1964

New York fans thought Y.A. Tittle was too old when he joined the team. Tittle shocked them by becoming the league's best passer and leading the Giants to the **NFL Championship Game** three years in a row. In 1963, he set an NFL record with 36 touchdown passes.

FRAN TARKENTON — Quarterback

- BORN: 2/3/1940   • PLAYED FOR TEAM: 1967 TO 1971

In the years between their championships in the 1960s and 1980s, the Giants' best player was Fran Tarkenton. He was picked to play in the **Pro Bowl** in four of his five years with New York. Tarkenton was the NFL's top-rated passer in 1969.

LEFT: Mel Hein
RIGHT: Fran Tarkenton

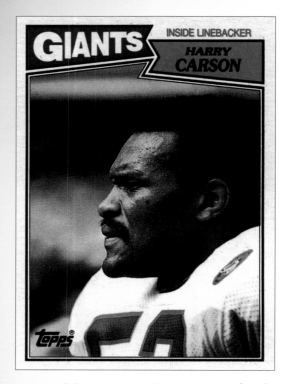

HARRY CARSON — Linebacker

- BORN: 11/26/1953
- PLAYED FOR TEAM: 1976 TO 1988

Harry Carson was a fierce tackler on the field and a gentleman off of it. He served as the defensive captain of the great New York teams of the 1980s. Carson was voted into the **Hall of Fame** in 2006.

PHIL SIMMS — Quarterback

- BORN: 11/3/1954
- PLAYED FOR TEAM: 1979 TO 1993

Phil who? That's the question that every New York fan asked when Phil Simms was drafted out of tiny Morehead State University. Simms made them remember his name by becoming a great leader. When he retired, he owned almost every team passing record.

LAWRENCE TAYLOR — Linebacker

- BORN: 2/4/1959   • PLAYED FOR TEAM: 1981 TO 1993

Along with Harry Carson and Carl Banks, Lawrence Taylor formed one of the best linebacking crews in history. "L.T." was like a human wrecking ball. He was so fast and aggressive—and so unpredictable—that opponents had to change their playbook when they faced the Giants.

ELI MANNING — Quarterback

- BORN: 1/3/1981 • FIRST YEAR WITH TEAM: 2004

For many years, Eli Manning played in the shadow of his older brother, Peyton. But before long, he developed into one of the NFL's best quarterbacks. Manning led the Giants to two Super Bowl victories, and he was named MVP of both games.

JASON PIERRE-PAUL — Defensive Lineman

- BORN: 1/1/1989 • FIRST YEAR WITH TEAM: 2010

Jason Pierre-Paul did not play football until his junior year in high school. Six years later, he was the defensive star of New York's championship team. In 2011, Pierre-Paul used his size, speed, and energy to record 16.5 **sacks**—the fourth-highest total in team history.

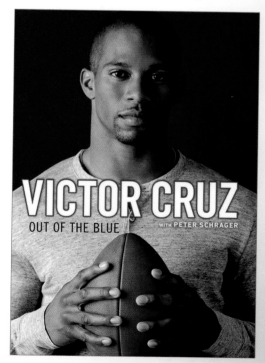

VICTOR CRUZ — Receiver

- BORN: 11/11/1986
- FIRST YEAR WITH TEAM: 2011

Victor Cruz grew up in New Jersey rooting for the Giants. Playing for them was a dream come true. In his first season, Cruz set the team record for receiving yards. After every touchdown, he thrilled New York fans by celebrating with his "salsa dance."

LEFT: Harry Carson   **RIGHT**: Victor Cruz

23

Calling the Shots

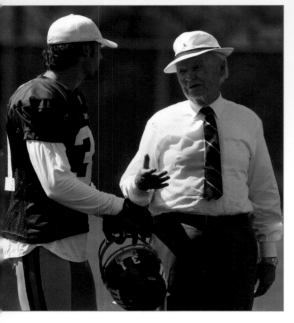

The through all the Giants' ups and downs, the Mara family has been overseeing the team's fortunes. Tim's son Wellington was a water boy for the Giants in the 1920s and eventually became team owner. The next generation of Maras, including Timothy and John, were in charge for the team's second, third and fourth Super Bowl wins.

The Maras have always been able to spot great leaders. From 1933 to 1946, coach Steve Owen guided New York to first place eight times. He was a true football pioneer. Owen invented the **safety blitz** and made the field goal into a popular weapon. He was also the first coach to move groups of players in and out of games to keep them fresh.

The coach who followed Owen was Jim Lee Howell. His greatest strength was his keen eye for talent. Howell made Tom Landry his defensive coach and Vince Lombardi his offensive coach. Landry

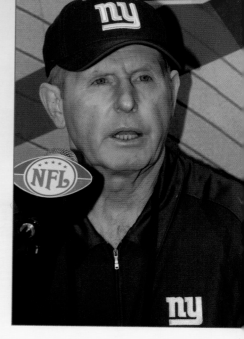

and Lombardi went on to become two of the greatest head coaches in NFL history.

The Giants have found many other good coaches over the years, including Allie Sherman and Jim Fassel. Sherman led the team to first-place finishes each season from 1961 to 1963. Fassel led the Giants to their third Super Bowl, in 2000. Their greatest victory that season was a 41–0 win over the Minnesota Vikings for the championship of the **National Football Conference (NFC)**.

Bill Parcells and Tom Coughlin guided the Giants to two Super Bowl titles each. They were longtime friends who shared a passion for hard work and winning. Parcells built a championship team around a group of hard-hitting linebackers. He demanded that his players be in peak condition and that they give everything they have on every play. Coughlin always found a way to get his players to believe in themselves. Both of his Super Bowl teams struggled during the regular season, only to gain confidence as they won difficult playoff games.

One Great Day

When the Giants took the field for Super Bowl XXI, they hoped to win their first championship in 30 seasons. New York had a fast and furious defense, good **special teams**, and a powerful offense. The team's leader was its quarterback, Phil Simms.

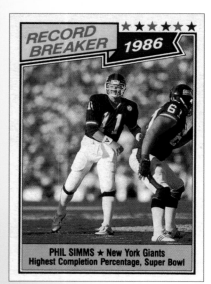

PHIL SIMMS ★ New York Giants
Highest Completion Percentage, Super Bowl

For Simms, it had been a bumpy road to the Super Bowl. When the team drafted him in 1979, many New York fans were angry. They had never even heard of Simms! During his first few years with the Giants, he was frequently injured, booed, and benched. But Simms never lost his confidence, and the experience made him an amazing **competitor**.

The Denver Broncos found out just how amazing he was in January of 1987. As Simms warmed up before the game, he had a big smile on his face. He told his teammates, "I've got it today!"

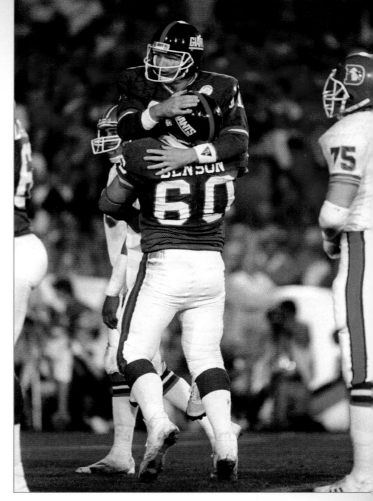

LEFT: This trading card celebrates Phil Simms's great day.
RIGHT: Brad Benson lifts Simms after one of his three touchdown passes in Super Bowl XXI.

Simms looked for holes in the Denver defense in the first half. He passed for a touchdown, while the New York defense kept the Broncos in check. In the second half, Simms was practically perfect. The Broncos could not stop him. At one point, he completed 10 passes in a row. Simms threw touchdown passes to Mark Bavaro and Phil McConkey. He also led the Giants to two other touchdowns and a field goal. The final score was 39–20.

After the game, Simms could hardly believe his own numbers. He had completed 22 of 25 passes for 268 yards and three touchdowns. The quarterback who could do nothing right when he came to New York could do no wrong on this day. "After all I've taken over the years," he said, "this makes everything worth it."

Legend Has It

Who started the NFL's "victory shower" celebration?

LEGEND HAS IT that New York nose tackle Jim Burt did. But it was teammate Harry Carson who turned the victory shower into a football *tradition*. Burt, who spent eight seasons with the Giants, doused coach Bill Parcells with a bucket of Gatorade for the first time after a win by the team in 1985. Carson loved the idea and took the lead on all future celebrations. Sometimes, he would even disguise himself on the sidelines so Parcells would not see him coming. Today, every football coach expects to get wet after a big win.

ABOVE: Harry Carson surprises Bill Parcells with a Gatorade shower.

Was the football term "Red Dog" started by the Giants?

LEGEND HAS IT that it was. "Red Dog" is another name for a blitz—a surprise play when the defense sends extra players across the **line of scrimmage**. It was named for Don "Red" Ettinger, who played for the Giants from 1948 to 1950. Ettinger once explained that his job was to "dog" the quarterback when he blitzed. The Giants started calling their blitz "Red Dog," and the name just caught on.

Did the Giants win a championship using basketball equipment?

LEGEND HAS IT that they did. On a bitterly cold day in 1934, the Giants met the Chicago Bears in New York for the NFL title. A sheet of ice covered the field. Neither team could gain good footing with their metal cleats. At halftime, the Giants turned to equipment manager Abe Cohen. He found nine pairs of rubber-bottomed basketball shoes at a local college. He gave them to the players, and they did the rest. New York scored 27 points in the fourth quarter, including two touchdowns by Ken Strong, to win the "Sneaker Game" by a score of 30–13.

It Really Happened

At the start of every NFL season, 32 teams can say that they are unbeaten. At the end of the year, it is a rare thing for any team to stay that way. In 1934 and 1942, the Chicago Bears were "perfect" in the regular season, but they failed to win the championship both times. In 1972, the Miami Dolphins went 14–0 and then won three times in the postseason, including the Super Bowl. They became the NFL's first undefeated team.

In 2007, the New England Patriots won all 16 of their games during the regular season. Their final victory was a narrow 38–35 win over the Giants. The game did not make a difference in the **standings**, but it was important to both clubs. The Patriots were able to keep their winning streak alive. The Giants learned that they were good enough to beat New England.

Even so, when the teams met again later that season in Super Bowl XLII, few experts believed the Giants had a chance to win. New York had barely survived three playoff battles leading up to the big game. Meanwhile, the Patriots were looking better and better. The key for the Giants was putting pressure on quarterback Tom Brady.

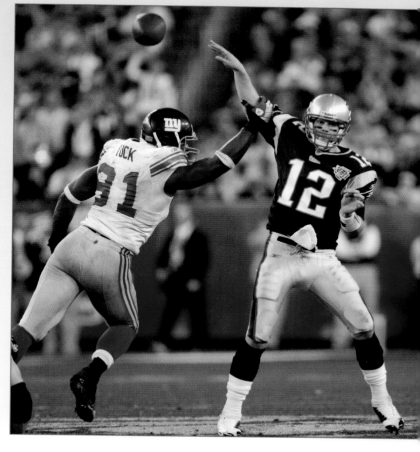

After three quarters, New England led 7–3. Early in the fourth quarter, the Giants went ahead when Eli Manning threw a touchdown pass to David Tyree. A few minutes later, Brady fired a short touchdown pass to give the lead back to the Patriots.

The Giants got the ball back for a final drive. All seemed lost as the Patriots swarmed around Manning. He desperately searched for an open receiver. Somehow, he spun out of trouble and launched a long pass to Tyree, who trapped the ball against his helmet as he fell to the turf. Four plays later, Manning flipped a pass to Plaxico Burress in the end zone to win the game 17–14. NFL fans would have to wait for the next perfect season. But until then, they would have the memory of one of football's greatest games.

Team Spirit

Fans of the Giants are as much a part of the team's proud history as the players and coaches. They have always been there to support Big Blue. Finding a spare ticket for a New York home game is next to impossible.

The seats at a Giants game are filled with fans wearing the jerseys of their favorite New York football heroes. Sometimes it looks like thousands of players are sitting in the stands. There aren't many fans who can match the noise they make. They love the team's stadium, which is one of the largest and loudest in the NFL.

After each of the team's Super Bowl victories, New York City has thrown a huge parade for the players and coaches. But fans in New Jersey think of the Giants as their home team, too. So the team has also treated them to big championship celebrations at its stadium in the Meadowlands.

LEFT: A fan roots for the Giants at Super Bowl XLVI.
ABOVE: Giants fans stuck this decal on their car windows in the 1960s.

Timeline

In this timeline, each Super Bowl is listed under the year it was played. Remember that the Super Bowl is held early in the year and is actually part of the previous season. For example, Super Bowl XLVI was played on February 5, 2012, but it was the championship of the 2011 NFL season.

1934
The Giants win the NFL title in the famous "Sneaker Game."

1925
The Giants join the NFL.

1929
Benny Friedman sets an NFL record with 20 touchdown passes.

1956
The Giants win their fourth NFL championship.

1963
Y.A. Tittle is named NFL MVP.

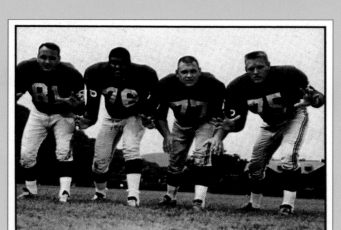

The Giants' defensive "front four" poses for a photo in the 1950s.

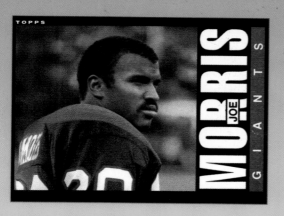

Joe Morris
starred for the
1987 champions.

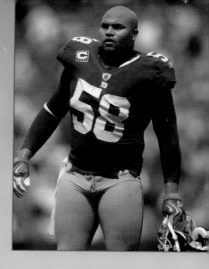

Antonio Pierce
helped the Giants
win in 2008.

2001
Michael Strahan sets
an NFL record with
22.5 sacks.

1987
The Giants win their
first Super Bowl.

2008
The Giants win their
third Super Bowl.

1981
Lawrence Taylor is
named **All-Pro** in his
rookie year.

1991
The Giants win their
second Super Bowl.

2012
The Giants win their
fourth Super Bowl.

Ahmad Bradshaw
was a star for the
2012 champs.

35

THE DUKE

For more than 25 years, the official NFL football had "The Duke" printed on its side. That was the nickname of Giants owner Wellington Mara. After Mara died in 2006, the NFL began using a new football with those same words on the side.

TRIPLE THREAT

In a 2011 game, Jason Pierre-Paul became the first NFL player with a sack, forced **fumble**, and blocked field goal in the same game.

FRANK
GIFFORD
NEW YORK GIANTS
HALFBACK

ARMED AND DANGEROUS

Frank Gifford could do it all as a runner, receiver, and defensive back for the Giants. He also got the job done as a passer. Gifford threw 14 passes for touchdowns during his career—the most ever for a non-quarterback.

GOING THE DISTANCE

In 2011, Victor Cruz scored a 99-yard touchdown after catching a pass from Eli Manning. Cruz broke the team record of 94 yards, set by Homer Jones in 1966.

MR. 200

In a 1949 game against the Chicago Bears, running back Gene "Choo Choo" Roberts caught four passes for 201 yards. Three weeks later, he caught seven passes against the Green Bay Packers and gained 212 yards. He is the only running back in history with two 200-yard receiving days.

TRUE VALUE

When Lawrence Taylor was named NFL MVP in 1986, it was just the fourth time in history that a defensive player won the award.

LEFT: Frank Gifford strikes a passing pose.
ABOVE: Victor Cruz and Hakeem Nicks signed this photo of a touchdown celebration in 2011.

Talking Football

"A Hall of Famer doesn't quit. A Hall of Famer realizes the crime is not being knocked down. The crime is not getting up again."

▶ *Lawrence Taylor, on the meaning of greatness*

"I like linebackers. I collect them. You can't have too many good ones."

▶ *Bill Parcells, on his favorite defensive players*

"I dreamed of this moment. I dreamed of this time. This is the best feeling of my life. I want to catch some *confetti*. I want to bring it home."

▶ *Victor Cruz, on winning Super Bowl XLVI*

"Guys like Charley Conerly, Y.A. Tittle, and Rosie Brown were truly my brothers during those years of frozen fields, broken bones, and championship triumphs."

▶ *Frank Gifford, on the feeling of family among the Giants in the 1950s and 1960s*

"This isn't about one person. It's about one team, a team coming together."
► *Eli Manning, on winning his second Super Bowl MVP*

"When I watch JPP play, it just makes me shake my head."
► *Justin Tuck, on the awesome talent of Jason Pierre-Paul*

"Our team feeds off the crowd, and we have been able to energize the crowd with our performance."
► *Tom Coughlin, on why the Giants do well when the fans stand up and cheer*

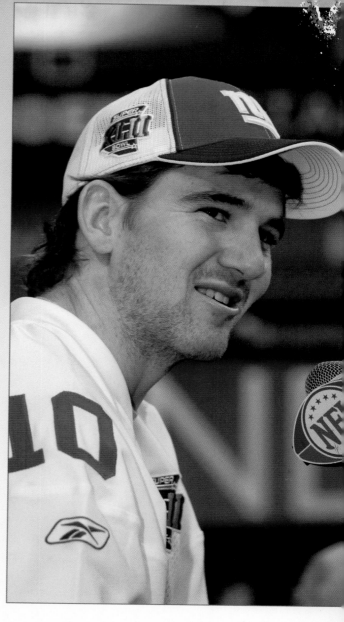

"Mentally and physically, Phil Simms was the toughest guy on this team."
► *Phil McConkey, on the quarterback of the Super Bowl XXI champions*

ABOVE: Eli Manning

Great Debates

People who root for the Giants love to compare their favorite moments, teams, and players. Some debates have been going on for years! How would you settle these classic football arguments?

The 1986 Giants would beat the 2011 Giants in a Super Bowl ...

OUTSIDE LINEBACKER
GIANTS
CARL BANKS
58

... because they had great balance. That season, Phil Simms threw for more than 3,000 yards, Joe Morris ran for more than 1,500 yards, and five players caught more than 20 passes. And the defense was even better! The Giants intercepted 24 passes that year. Lawrence Taylor, Carl Banks (LEFT), and Leonard Marshall combined for 39 sacks. The 1986 Giants could beat teams in a dozen different ways.

Really? The 2011 Giants had an unstoppable Super Bowl weapon ...

... and his name was Eli Manning. When things looked their worst, Manning was at his best. Manning had two great receivers in Hakeem Nicks and Victor Cruz, who could turn short gains into long touchdowns. It takes a total team effort to win a championship, but the 2011 Giants had a major advantage because Manning always came up big with the pressure on.

Frank Gifford was the team's greatest all-around player ...

... because he could do it all on a football field. During the 1950s, Gifford was one of the NFL's best runners and also a top defensive back. At a time when most stars specialized in offense or defense, he was an excellent "two-way" player. In 1960, Gifford suffered an injury that kept him out until 1962. He returned as a receiver at age 32. Over the next three seasons, he caught 110 passes, including 17 touchdowns.

Gifford's not even in the top two ...

... because in the days when everyone was a two-way player, the Giants had two of the best in Ken Strong (**RIGHT**) and Ward Cuff. Strong was excellent in every part of the game—from blocking to kicking to running to passing. He retired after breaking his back in 1939, but he returned in 1944 as a kicker and helped the Giants finish in first place twice. By then, Cuff was the star of the team. No one was tougher on offense or defense. He was one of the NFL's best pass defenders, kickers, runners, and receivers.

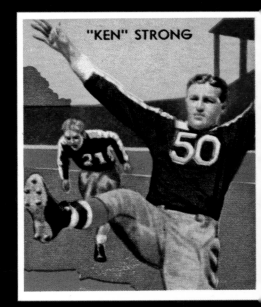

"KEN" STRONG

For the Record

The great Giants teams and players have left their marks on the record books. These are the "best of the best" ...

Charley Conerly

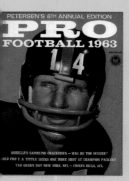

Y.A. Tittle

GIANTS AWARD WINNERS

WINNER	AWARD	YEAR
Mel Hein	NFL Most Valuable Player	1938
Frank Gifford	Pro Bowl co-MVP	1959
Charley Conerly	NFL Most Valuable Player	1959
Allie Sherman	Coach of the Year	1961
Allie Sherman	Coach of the Year	1962
Y.A. Tittle	NFL Most Valuable Player	1963
Lawrence Taylor	Defensive Rookie of the Year	1981
Lawrence Taylor	Defensive Player of the Year	1981
Lawrence Taylor	Defensive Player of the Year	1982
Phil Simms	Pro Bowl MVP	1986
Lawrence Taylor	Defensive Player of the Year	1986
Bill Parcells	Coach of the Year	1986
Lawrence Taylor	NFL Most Valuable Player	1986
Phil Simms	Super Bowl XXI MVP	1987
Ottis Anderson	Super Bowl XXV MVP	1991
Dan Reeves	Coach of the Year	1993
Jim Fassel	Coach of the Year	1997
Michael Strahan	Defensive Player of the Year	2001
Eli Manning	Super Bowl XLII MVP	2008
Eli Manning	Super Bowl XLVI MVP	2012

GIANTS ACHIEVEMENTS

ACHIEVEMENT	YEAR
NFL Champions	1927
NFL Eastern Division Champions	1933
NFL Eastern Division Champions	1934
NFL Champions	1934
NFL Eastern Division Champions	1935
NFL Eastern Division Champions	1938
NFL Champions	1938
NFL Eastern Division Champions	1939
NFL Eastern Division Champions	1941
NFL Eastern Division Champions	1944
NFL Eastern Division Champions	1946
NFL Eastern Division Champions	1956
NFL Champions	1956
NFL Eastern Division Champions	1958
NFL Eastern Division Champions	1959
NFL Eastern Conference Champions	1961
NFL Eastern Conference Champions	1962
NFL Eastern Conference Champions	1963
NFC East Champions	1986
NFC Champions	1986
Super Bowl XXI Champions	1986*
NFC East Champions	1989
NFC East Champions	1990
NFC Champions	1990
Super Bowl XXV Champions	1990*
NFC East Champions	1997
NFC East Champions	2000
NFC Champions	2000
NFC East Champions	2005
Super Bowl XLII Champions	2007*
NFC East Champions	2008
NFC Champions	2010
Super Bowl XLVI Champions	2011*

Super Bowls are played early the following year, but the game is counted as the championship of this season.

ABOVE: Amani Toomer starred for the Super Bowl XLII champs.
BELOW: Super Bowl XLVI star Hakeem Nicks signed this photo of a touchdown catch.

The history of a football team is made up of many smaller stories. These stories take place all over the map—not just in the city a team calls "home." Match the pushpins on these maps to the **Team Facts**, and you will begin to see the story of the Giants unfold!

TEAM FACTS

1 East Rutherford, New Jersey—*The Giants have played here since 1976.*

2 Winthrop, Massachusetts—*Mark Bavaro was born here.*

3 Indianapolis, Indiana—*The Giants won Super Bowl XLVI here.*

4 Fort Bragg, North Carolina—*Joe Morris was born here.*

5 Tampa, Florida—*The Giants won Super Bowl XXV here.*

6 New Orleans, Louisiana—*Eli Manning was born here.*

7 Houston, Texas—*Michael Strahan was born here.*

8 Ada, Oklahoma—*Jeremy Shockey was born here.*

9 Pasadena, California—*The Giants won Super Bowl XXI here.*

10 Glendale, Arizona—*The Giants won Super Bowl XLII here.*

11 Lebanon, Kentucky—*Phil Simms was born here.*

12 London, England—*Osi Umenyiora was born here.*

Mark Bavaro

45

Glossary

🧠 **ALL-AROUND**—Good at many different parts of the game.

🧠 **ALL-PRO**—An honor given to the best players at their positions at the end of each season.

🧠 **COMPETITOR**—Someone who has a strong desire to win.

🧠 **CONFETTI**—Small pieces of colored paper.

🧠 **DECADES**—Periods of 10 years; also specific periods, such as the 1950s.

🧠 **FIELD GOAL**—A goal from the field, kicked over the crossbar and between the goal posts. A field goal is worth three points.

🧠 **FUMBLE**—A ball that is dropped by the player carrying it.

🧠 **GENERATION**—A period of years roughly equal to the time it takes for a person to be born, grow up, and have children.

🧠 **HALL OF FAME**—The museum in Canton, Ohio, where football's greatest players are honored. A player voted into the Hall of Fame is sometimes called a "Hall of Famer."

🧠 **LINE OF SCRIMMAGE**—The imaginary line that separates the offense and defense before each play begins.

🧠 **LOGO**—A symbol or design that represents a company or team.

🧠 **MOST VALUABLE PLAYER (MVP)**—The award given each year to the league's best player; also given to the best player in the Super Bowl and Pro Bowl.

🧠 **NATIONAL FOOTBALL CONFERENCE (NFC)**—One of two groups of teams that make up the NFL. The winner of the NFC plays the winner of the American Football Conference (AFC) in the Super Bowl.

🧠 **NATIONAL FOOTBALL LEAGUE (NFL)**—The league that started in 1920 and is still operating today.

🧠 **NFL CHAMPIONSHIP GAME**—The game played to decide the winner of the league each year from 1933 to 1969.

🧠 **PLAYOFFS**—The games played after the regular season to determine which teams play in the Super Bowl.

🧠 **POSTSEASON**—Another term for playoffs.

🧠 **PRO BOWL**—The NFL's all-star game, played after the regular season.

🧠 **PROFESSIONAL**—A player or team that plays a sport for money.

🧠 **REMARKABLE**—Unusual or exceptional.

🧠 **ROOKIE**—A player in his first season.

🧠 **SACKS**—Tackles of the quarterback behind the line of scrimmage.

🧠 **SAFETY BLITZ**—A defensive play in which a safety blasts through the offensive line on the snap of the ball.

🧠 **SPECIAL TEAMS**—The groups of players who take the field for punts, kickoffs, field goals, and extra points.

🧠 **STANDINGS**—A list of teams, starting with the team with the best record and ending with the team with the worst record.

🧠 **SUPER BOWL**—The championship of the NFL, played between the winners of the NFC and AFC.

🧠 **TRADITION**—A belief or custom that is handed down from generation to generation.

🧠 **VERSATILE**—Able to do many things well.

OVERTIME

TEAM SPIRIT introduces a great way to stay up to date with your team! Visit our **OVERTIME** link and get connected to the latest and greatest updates. **OVERTIME** serves as a young reader's ticket to an exclusive web page—with more stories, fun facts, team records, and photos of the Giants. Content is updated during and after each season. The **OVERTIME** feature also enables readers to send comments and letters to the author! Log onto:

www.norwoodhousepress.com/library.aspx

and click on the tab: **TEAM SPIRIT** to access **OVERTIME**.

Read all the books in the series to learn more about professional sports. For a complete listing of the baseball, basketball, football, and hockey teams in the **TEAM SPIRIT** series, visit our website at:

www.norwoodhousepress.com/library.aspx

On the Road

NEW YORK GIANTS
MetLife Stadium
20 Murray Hill Parkway
East Rutherford, New Jersey 07073
201-935-8111
www.giants.com

THE PRO FOOTBALL HALL OF FAME
2121 George Halas Drive NW
Canton, Ohio 44708
330-456-8207
www.profootballhof.com

On the Bookshelf

To learn more about the sport of football, look for these books at your library or bookstore:

- Frederick, Shane. *The Best of Everything Football Book.* North Mankato, Minnesota: Capstone Press, 2011.

- Jacobs, Greg. *The Everything Kids' Football Book: The All-Time Greats, Legendary Teams, Today's Superstars—And Tips on Playing Like a Pro.* Avon, Massachusetts: Adams Media Corporation, 2010.

- Editors of *Sports Illustrated for Kids. 1st and 10: Top 10 Lists of Everything in Football.* New York, New York: Sports Illustrated Books, 2011.

About the Author

MARK STEWART has written more than 50 books on football and over 150 sports books for kids. He grew up in New York City during the 1960s rooting for the Giants and Jets, and was lucky enough to meet players from both teams. Mark comes from a family of writers. His grandfather was Sunday Editor of *The New York Times,* and his mother was Articles Editor of *Ladies' Home Journal* and *McCall's.* Mark has profiled hundreds of athletes over the past 25 years. He has also written several books about his native New York and New Jersey, his home today. Mark is a graduate of Duke University, with a degree in history. He lives and works in a home overlooking Sandy Hook, New Jersey. You can contact Mark through the Norwood House Press website.

M.   10-15